Super Sharks

Written by Ben Hubbard

Collins

Sharks are the super hunters of the sea.

2

They prowl with speed and rule the world beneath the waves.

Some sharks like mild seas.
They swim in the tropics.

Others are at home in freezing seas.

Some sharks travel around to seek out new prey.

Sharks come in lots of shapes and colours.
Some have a green glow.
Others are brown, or blue with spots.

Some sharks are grey with heads
like hammers.

Sharks use their fins and tails to help them swim with speed.

fins

tail

They have powerful jaws to crunch their food.

Some sharks are born with rows of pointed teeth. Their teeth are sharp like saws.

When a tooth falls out, a new one grows in.

A snooping shark uses its head and snout to test if prey is food. It can graze, collide or sweep past its prey ...

then it strikes!

Tiger sharks are some of the most feared sharks on Earth.

They prowl in groups to kill their prey.

Frilled sharks are one of the world's deep sea sharks.

They stay near the sea bed.

Sharks are wild. They swim around looking for prey to scoop up.

If a shark fin appears in the sea, don't be afraid to start back to the beach.

Lots of sharks are caught in nets. This means the number of sharks is getting smaller.

We should not fear sharks. They are not monsters. People should protect sharks, so they continue to rule the waves.

Sharks

After reading

Letters and Sounds: Phase 5

Word count: 247

Focus phonemes: /igh/ i, i-e /ai/ ay, ey, a-e /oa/ o, ow, o-e /oo/ ue, ew, u-e /ee/ ea /ow/ ou /oo/ oul /or/ aw, augh, al /er/ or, ear /e/ a /u/ o, our, o-e

Common exception words: are, so, their, people, be, of, the, to, we, have, when, one

Curriculum links: Science: Animal habitats

National Curriculum learning objectives: Reading/word reading: apply phonic knowledge and skills as the route to decode words; read accurately by blending sounds in unfamiliar words containing GPCs that have been taught; read other words of more than one syllable that contain taught GPCs; read aloud accurately books that are consistent with their developing phonic knowledge; re-read books to build up their fluency and confidence in word reading; Reading/comprehension: link what they have read or hear read to their own experiences; discuss word meanings; discuss the significance of the title and event

Developing fluency

- Practise reading the common exception words fluently. Look through the book and find the following common exception words together: **are**, **so**, **their**, **people**, **be**, **of**, **the**, **to**.
- Take turns to read a page each with your child. Model reading fluently.

Phonic practice

- Look through the book. Challenge your child to find words that have the /ee/ sound in them. (*sea, speed, freezing, green, teeth, beach, sweep, deep, means*)
- How many words can they think of that rhyme with **jaw**? (e.g. *saw, paw, claw, raw*)

Extending vocabulary

- Ask your child:
  - What does the word **prowl** mean? (e.g. *creep around looking for prey*)
  - On page 10 the author describes sharks' teeth as **sharp**. What other words could you use to describe sharks' teeth? (e.g. *pointy, spiky*)